Mary Lou,

Love Letters from Jesus

Kisses from Heaven's Best

We are blessed to know the Best! May these letters help you to know even more how much He LOVES YOU!!

me too! Sally

Sally F. Boenau

Love Letters from Jesus

Kisses from Heaven's Best

Copyright © 2013 Sally F. Boenau

ISBN:1492711136
ISBN-13:9781492711131

Not to be copied for commercial use or personal gain. Consent from the publisher for personal use and encouragement of others is given.

spiritandlifelighters@gmail.com

Published by:

Spirit and Life Lighters

122 S Greenbriar Woods Rd

Hendersonville, NC 28739

Bible quotes found in this book are from the King James Version of the Bible

First Printing : 2013

TABLE OF CONTENTS

TABLE OF CONTENTS

INTRODUCTION

Jesus says His words are spirit and life. (John 6:33) Many years ago, those words sank into my heart as the truth, so I began to give my attention to the 'words in red' in the Bible. It has been a journey of growing in understanding and revelation of what they mean and applying them in my daily life. Though I have been far from perfect in my pursuit and have many miles yet to travel, I would not trade this path I've chosen for anything in this world.

A woman with a blood disorder sought Jesus with faith that he could cure her when no one else could. (Luke 8:43-48) As her faith drew healing virtue from Him, so I have found countless virtues flow from Him through His words received and held on to in faith in my heart.

The idea of love letters popped into my mind one day, and, knowing that He is the Alpha and Omega, I believed I could find virtues from A to Z in Him. These letters are for the many believers who need affirmation, inspiration and encouragement. They 'light up' and 'water' the hope of the glorious, unending life ahead with Him in heaven as well as how pleased He and His Father are with the choice to live out the virtues of love here on earth. These letters are my personal response to His command to 'feed His sheep.'
Every child of God, including you, is very precious and valuable to Him and important in His Kingdom.

Remember, You are loved by the Lord above All !

Prayer for Abundance

Dear Father of Abundance,
I ask that this precious child of yours, who I love and have bought with my blood, experience the law of spirit and life in me which overcomes the spirit of sin and death. Help them to recognize and reject the deception of the darkness even when it masquerades as an angel of light or a minister of righteousness. Lead them on the glorious path of light, love, trust and forgiveness as you led me.
Jesus

Abundant Scriptures

John 10:10
Matthew 7:11
Luke 23:38-43
Matthew 4:24
Romans 1:18-21
Ephesians 2:10
James 1:5-8

Abundance

Beloved,

I so desire to share my abundant life and love with you today. When you ask the Father in faith, with nothing wavering, you can be sure you will receive what you need. When the thief on the cross next to mine asked to be with me, I told him, 'Today, you will be with me in paradise.' And he is.

My abundant life on earth included water walking, healing the sick, raising the dead and dying on a cross. All these things were done through faith in and obedience to our Father's will. There are 'good works' and ample provision for you, too, as you trust and obey His leading. Every time you give your all, like the widow or invest your talents on my behalf while maintaining a humble heart, you are truly rich in the kingdom of God.

Creation itself provides a sense of abundant life that costs you nothing. A beautiful sunrise, majestic mountains, the song of a bird, a baby's smile - all these treasures come from God, the Father, and were created for your pleasure as well as His. Truly, the very act of loving God with all your heart, mind, soul and strength will honor Him and fill your heart with joy and peace. Try it right now... you'll see.

Abundantly yours,

Jesus

Prayer for God's Adopted

Dear Father God,
This is a special child of yours who loves you so much. May they be the beneficiary of all your blessings and your supremacy that keep them from being plucked from your hand
by anything or anyone.
Thank you that they are free from the spirit of bondage that would bind them in fear so they can be free to worship you in spirit and truth all the days of their life.
Jesus

Scriptures for His Adopted

John 15:16
Mark 15:34
Hebrews 12:2
Colossians 1:19-23
John 14:3
Matthew 28:1-7
Ephesians 3:14-19

Adopted

Dear Child of the King,

"I have chosen you..." - my words of spirit and life to you today and every day. Adoption carries within it a choice-a deliberate decision and desire to be related.

Often, before the joy of adoption, there is the pain of abandonment and rejection. Even though I am the only begotten Son of God, I experienced that pain and anguish for you as I hung on the cross, apparently abandoned by not only man but God. My cry, "My God, my God, why has thou forsaken me?" was real. However, remember my Father's response was resurrection and fulfillment of the joy He set before me which is having brothers and sisters like you with whom I can share eternity.

My sacrifice opened the door of adoption for you and it was well worth it to me. I love being able to present you holy, unblameable and irreproachable before our Father. I so look forward to coming back for you so that we can be together forever. Even now the Spirit is present working in you to prepare you as my bride. Look for His gifts and fruit to manifest in you and flow through you.

Be Expectant!
Jesus

Prayer for His Beautiful One

Dear Creator of Real Beauty,
You are especially fond of this beautiful child of yours. They are growing more like us all the time. May You continually draw them to our throne of grace, for I know that there is where they will find help - for themselves and for others - in their times of need.
Jesus

Beautiful Scriptures

John 1:4
1 John 2:15-17
Isaiah 53:4-6
1 Peter 2:24-25
Matthew 11:28-30
Matthew 8:5-13
Hebrews 4:14-16

Beautiful

Dear Beautiful One,

"Beauty is in the eye of the beholder" and , as God, the Father and I behold you, we see you beautiful. The world's definition of beauty is very different from ours, but ours is true and lasting and includes all of you - inside and outside. Your choice not to cherish the world and its fame and fortune above your heavenly Father and His word is a wise one that will gain you eternal rewards.

The Father and I made you and are pleased with what we see. I know the scars and mars that may appear to the natural eye, but all of those have been borne on my cross so now we see you as you are truly meant to be.

If you will look upon me with the eyes of your spirit, you will see how deeply I love you just the way you are. My eye is single and my gaze is upon what a beauty you are!

Will you rest in the joy you are to me alone?

Forever in love,
Jesus

Prayer for the Believer

Dear Creator of All,
I know how the faith of this precious one pleases you and I also know of your promise to reward them for seeking you wholeheartedly. May you encourage and affirm them in their faith just as I praised the centurion who was so confident in my ability to heal his servant.
Jesus

Believing Scriptures

Matthew 8:4-12
John 14:1-3 & 12
John 8:1-11
Luke 12:32
1 Corinthians 2:9
1 John 5:14
Hebrews 12:28
Romans 8:6

Believing

Dear Believing One,

You cannot even imagine what a pleasure it is to look forward to our being together forever. Just think what fun and excitement you've experienced planning that special party or finding that perfect gift for a loved one in your life. That is only a hint of my joy in making arrangements for your mansion in heaven.

I am also just as pleased and joyful as you live and move and have your being in the spirit of believing in me. I really meant it when I told you and my disciples that you need not fear, for it's our Father's good pleasure to give you the kingdom. He truly has awesome and amazing things awaiting all who love and obey him.

My believing in what our Father told me to do included healing the sick, feeding a crowd and offering forgiveness as well as being rejected by the religious and political leaders of the day and being deserted and betrayed by those closest to me. The power of the Spirit brought me through and raised me from the dead. And this same Spirit is with you always, so you can enjoy the peace and life there is in being spiritually minded and you can walk in the newness of our kingdom in your heart

Thankfully yours,

Jesus

Prayer for the Brilliant One

Dear Source of True Light,
I praise you, God, Father of life, light and love.
I ask for an increased awareness and acceptance
of the guidance and power of the Holy Spirit in
this precious one's life. May their brilliance be ever
increasing until that day they join us in our kingdom.
Jesus

Brilliant Scriptures

Matthew 5:24
Ephesians 6:12
Matthew 5:16
Luke 11:13
John 8:32
Romans 2:29
Romans 8:14

Brilliant

Dear Bright One,

'You are the light of the world.' I might add that you are light in my world as well as this one where there are rulers of darkness set against your shining.

While 'brilliant' is usually used to describe someone's natural intelligence or the excellence of an idea or an accomplishment, to our Father and me, it is how brightly your faith, hope and love illuminate your life as well as the lives of others. To us, IQ is not intelligence quotient but inspiration quickening.

I know you have experienced moments when the Holy Spirit inspired solutions to situations-big and small-in your spirit. Treasure and ask for more of these moments and your brilliance will increase as will the joy you bring to our hearts. Whether or not it is acknowledged or appreciated by those around you is not the measure of its influence or worth. God alone is the judge of that. As you are true to following my word and the Spirit, you will hear our words -

'Well done!'
Your Morningstar,
Jesus

Prayer for One Who Cares

Dearest Abba Father,

This caring one is precious to both of us. May they not grow weary but know that they are wired for love and that their spirit is renewed daily for the good works you've ordained for them. Let them know that you are in the renewing and rewarding business so they can be continually lively and expectant!

Jesus

Caring Scriptures

1 Peter 5:8-9
Genesis 2:15
John 13:34
Matthew 5:44-46 & 25:34-40
John 10:10
John 15:16
Galatians 6:2

Caring

Dear Caring One,

Each time you've cared for one of the 'little ones' that have crossed your path on earth, you have acted in my name and done it unto me. Both our Father and I are pleased. Your loving, blessing, praying for and doing good to others - even those who are not your friends - is worth more than silver and gold.

I wish to care for you today - both affectionally and watchfully - just as you care for others. I want you to cast all of your cares upon me and let me bear those burdens that weigh you down and rob you of your joy. Then you will be more able to bear the burdens of others thus fulfilling the 'law of Christ.'

As man's first assignment was to 'dress and keep the garden,' so mine is to care for you-and yours is to care for others. It's a choice - a two way street which holds no guarantee that the recipient of the care will respond in kind. But, I promise to show you that I care in a multitude of ways every day. Look for them, be blessed by them and pass them on.

I yearn for you to enjoy the abundance I came to bring in your 'garden of life.' I've ordained for you to bear fruit that will last. Will you trust me in this? You won't be disappointed if you do.

Affectionately yours,

Jesus

Prayer for His Chosen One

Dear Creator of Excellence,

This chosen one is such a joy to my heart. May your ear be ever open to their needs and desires as they delight themselves in thoughts of us and our kingdom and continue as my disciple. May they experience our peace which surpasses worldly knowledge as they grow in their knowledge of me as their way, truth and life.

Jesus

Chosen Scriptures

John 14:6 & 15:16
Ephesians 2:10
Luke 10:38-42
Matthew 7:24-25
Romans 5:17
Matthew 25:31-40
Galatians 5:22-23

Chosen

Dear Exceptional One,

I have chosen you and appointed you to bear fruit that will be lasting. There is no one else who can fulfill the purpose for which you were created. And that purpose is good says God who alone is the author of true goodness.

I told Mary, who chose to sit at my feet while dinner was being prepared, that she had chosen the good part and it would not be taken away from her. Likewise, your choice to pay attention to what I've said and live accordingly is the wisest decision you will ever make. You will experience an unbelievably meaningful life in this world as well as the next.

Right now it may seem that following me isn't that desirable. Can it produce real the wealth that the rich and famous seem to be enjoying? Just choosing to be kind may seem to be worthless compared to gaining the riches and praise of this world, but you will be surprised how that act of kindness given to a little one in the world's eyes gains you blessing and an inheritance that surpasses anything you can dream or imagine. And it will last forever.

Love, joy and peace - these are some of the delicious fruits ripening within you as you follow me. Real quality - that's who you are!

Jesus

Prayer for Comfort

Dear Source of All Comfort,
On the cross, you had me bear the grief, pain and sorrow as well as the sin if this precious child of yours. May they seek and find the reality and release of the total redemption that is theirs through my act of obedience. I died so they may live in the sufficiency of my grace. Surely, I established the 'law of Christ' by bearing their burdens and Paul told them they would fulfill it as they bear one another's.
Jesus

Comforting Scriptures

Matthew 11:28-30
Isaiah 53:4-5
Ephesians 3:14-21
2 Thessalonians 2:16-17
Luke 11:9
1 Peter 2:21-25
Revelations 21:4

Comfort

Dear Precious One,

Oh, how I yearn to bless and comfort you in your times of sadness and pain. Is your heart hurting and your mind attacked by 'why?' and 'if only?' Turn to me and seek my help. I earnestly desire you to be the beneficiary of my bearing your griefs and sorrows on the cross as well as being wounded for your sins.

My life on earth also included great sadness as I observed and experienced the powers of death and darkness at work. My faith in our Father and His plan of redemption and eternal life for you comforted and carried me through my life and death on earth as well as into His Kingdom where there is no crying, dying, sorrow or pain.

Cast your cares on me for I do care for you. And let my faith and trust in the Father and His will dwell in your heart so you will be able to endure to the end and be healed, delivered and preserved- safe and sound.

Forever yours in love,
Jesus

Prayer for the Courageous

Dear Father of Courage,

May this child be like Daniel in the lion's den,
trusting with all their heart that you are in
charge of their life, death, resurrection and
and everything in between.
No matter what happens, I know that not
a hair on their head shall perish.
Jesus

Scriptures of Courage

John 16:33
Isaiah 53:4-5
Romans 8:10-11
Revelations 2:1-3:18
John 11:25-26
Mark 11:24-25
John 10:27-30
Luke 21:17-19
Proverbs 3:5-8

Courage

Dear Brave Heart,

I know that there have been and are times when you feel helpless and hopeless. Remember, I am ever present to provide you with my strength and compassion in bearing your pain and sorrow. I have overcome the world and that same overcoming power is available to you in me. You bless me as you choose to not give up but to trust in me and go on. The rewards of the overcomer are greater than you can possibly imagine. You can check that out in the second and third chapters of Revelation.

As resurrection and eternal life in the Kingdom of Heaven were the Father's plan for me, so it is for you. Never doubt that His plan is different or His power insufficient to bring you through. He is greater than all, and no one can steal you from Him. Praise Him and pray in the spirit more and you will see great things.

Confidently and lovingly yours,
Jesus

Prayer for the Delivered One

Dear Deliverer,

Thank you for your faithfulness to deliver this loved one out of the hands of the enemy and all evil.

May they be filled with joy and expectancy of the glory of our kingdom which has no end.

Jesus

Scriptures for the Delivered One

Matthew 6:13
Luke 22:32
John 17:12
Romans 8:28-29
Hebrews 6:12
John 6:33
1 Corinthians 10:13

Delivered

Dear Redeemed One,

When I taught my disciples to pray, '...lead us not into temptation but deliver us from evil...,' I was providing our key to kingdom living on earth. As you put your trust in us for your very life, your deliverance becomes our responsibility and is assured. I prayed for Peter's faith not to fail and ultimately it did not. I pray for you, too. And as I kept my disciples, I keep you in more ways than you can even imagine.

Though it is every man's yearning to be trouble free, until I come again, the redemption I provide on earth is peace and freedom in, not always from tribulations.

I endured many trials and tests during my life on earth and have overcome the world with all its troubles. You will never be tried beyond your God given ability to endure. Indeed, it is in your overcoming tribulation that our Father's plan to conform you into my image is fulfilled.

Faith and patience will bring you through to every good thing He has promised you, the greatest of these being love and life eternal.

Your Redeemer Kinsman,

Jesus

Prayer for Endurance and Excellence

Dear Author of Excellence,

You alone know the beginning and the end for all, including this precious child of yours. May they receive by faith the reality of the eternal weight of glory which you have for them for enduring the pressures of this present world and remembering that they can cast all their cares on me because I truly care for them.

Jesus

Excellent and Enduring Scriptures

Mark 12:42-44
Matthew 24:8-13
Matthew 8:6
1 Corinthians 10:13 & 13:7
Matthew 11:28-30
James 5:11
1 Peter 2:18-20

Endurance and Excellence

Dear Heart,

'Don't quit!' How many times have you heard those words or have you spoken them to others? When heeded, there is hidden in them the promise of 'well done.' It is my joy to commend you when you have given your all, as I did to the woman who put her last cent in the offering plate while others were giving much more, but from their abundance.

I want you to know that I see every choice you make to endure in faith, love and patience rather than being offended or quitting. I desire for you to experience my presence in your heart as you walk in this most crucial and valuable aspect of love. 'Excellent,' our Father exclaims to each act of loving endurance you wholeheartedly bring to Him, in response to His command to 'bear, believe, hope and endure all things.'

Faithfully yours 'til the end / beginning,
Jesus

Prayer for the Faithful One

Faith-filled Father,

I pray for this loved one of yours and mine. May their faith kick out doubt and fear when faced with a need - their own or someone else's. May they realize that their faith, patience and love are what you are looking for to avenge them of their adversary.

Jesus

Faith Scriptures

Mark 2:1-12
John 6:63
Matthew 9:20-22
Matthew 8:5-13 & 15:22-29
Luke 18:1-8 & 8:41-56
Hebrews 11:6
Romans 5:1-5

Faith

Dear Faithful One,

Your faith in me brings great joy to my heart as my faith did to our Father's heart. There is no greater honor you can give to another than your faith in them. My words are spirit and life. As you believe and act on them you experience kingdom life.

'Your faith has made you whole.' I spoke this to the woman with a blood disorder which no one could cure. Her faith in me made her the beneficiary of my healing virtue. Then there was the centurion with a sick servant, the mother with the child oppressed by the devil, Jairus with a daughter on death's door and the group who raised the roof to get their paralyzed friend to me. All sought me in faith and all received what they desired. Your faith gains the same results whether you are the giver or the receiver.

There will be trials and tests in your life. Your unwavering faith in me will always bring my power on the scene and it will make you whole. Having the love of God shed abroad in your heart is one of the most awesome results of trial gone through faithfully.

Our Father is a rewarder of those who diligently seek Him. As you trust in His Word, the Holy Spirit and me, you can be sure that He will act with your best interest in mind, no matter what the situation is. He is good and supreme - ALL the time.

Faithfully yours always,

Jesus

Prayer for the Forgiver

Abba Father,

Thank you for forgiving my friend and adopting them as your child and betrothing them to me. May 'Abba Father' always be their cry - in times of triumph and temptation. Open their eyes wider and wider to the life of grace where forgiveness and mercy triumph over all condemnation.

Jesus

Forgiving Scriptures

Matthew 6:12
Mark 11:25-26
Luke 23:34
1 Peter 3:14 & 4:1-2
Ephesians 6:10-17
Romans 8:15
Hebrews 12:15

Forgiveness

Dear Precious One,

You hold the key to the throne room of God, where mercy and grace abound. 'Forgive them for they know not what they do,' are my living words before our Father for all the times you have missed it. They are also living words to help you escape judgment and the bitterness that defiles many. Every time you have chosen to forgive, you have pleased our Father and are a real overcomer.

When you forgive, you are not condoning or agreeing with evil. You are yielding your right to judge to the true Judge of all. Your trust in His judgment mirrors mine. Though you may suffer in the flesh (as I did), you will experience the love and peace that surpasses knowledge and the defeat of evil.

Please accept my forgiveness extended to you, and extend it to others. There is not a wicked way that our Father does not know about or can't handle.

Redeemed! How we love to declare and fulfill it.

Grace and peace to you,
Jesus

Freedom Prayer

All Knowing Father,
Guide this precious one of yours with your spirit as you did me. Thank you that as they follow me, they will experience my truth, and this truth will set them free to be all you have ordained them to be.
Jesus

Freedom Scriptures

Matthew 4:19 & 8:5-13
Acts 3:1-9
John 11:1-44
Luke 22:42-69
Mark 16:16-20
John 8:31-32
Luke 9:22-26

Freedom

Dear Liberated One,

It is a great day for me as well as for you when you realize you are free to follow me - and you do! There is nothing more exhilarating than living out in faith what the Father reveals to you through His Word and His Spirit. I'm sure you felt both the risk and reward as you read my experience with Lazarus when he fell sick and died. To hold on to my Father's will that the illness was not unto death but His glory and move accordingly was a choice. The presence of unbelief in all those around me did not prevail over my belief in my Father's will and power to raise Lazarus up. Nor was my choice to believe in His will and power any different when I submitted to betrayal and the cross. Two deaths, two resurrections; both with the same message of God's glory, power and goodness. One inspired belief in some and the other opened the door to salvation for many - and so much more.

Believe me when I tell you that it is just as life giving to you and others when you daily take up your cross to follow me as it is when you lay hands on the sick and they recover. Both bring glory to the Father and He is more than willing to reveal His will for your walking out both of these here on earth. Your confidence in your Father and me is a liberating force greater than all the armies of this world possess!

Freely yours,

Jesus

Prayer for the Giver

Dear Giver of All,
You have given this child of yours many gifts including righteousness and eternal life. May they truly experience the joy of being the giver as well as the receiver of your awesome gifts. I can testify to the fact that it is more blessed to give than to receive.
Jesus

Scriptures for Givers

Luke 6:38
Matthew 14:15-21
Matthew 17:24-27
1 Corinthians 2:9
Matthew 5:42 & 6:20-21
2 Corinthians 9:7-8
Acts 20:35
Hebrews 12:2

Giving Gladly

Dear Generous One,

'Give and it shall be given to you...' I spoke these words when I walked the earth, and they are just as real and true for you today as they were then.

I gave as my Father led me, people sought after me in faith and my heart was filled with compassion. Whether it was food for a crowd, money for taxes or healing from disease and oppression, there was always a generous supply and no reluctance on my part to give. For the joy set before me (which includes being with you forever), I ultimately gave my life on earth, but, oh, how much more I have received in return.

Though your eye cannot see nor can your heart conceive what the Father has in store for you because you love Him, I assure you it is beyond your greatest expectations. He is good and He loves a cheerful giver!

As Do I,
Jesus

Prayer for Grace

Dear Author of Grace,

This precious child of yours, chosen before the foundation of the world, will need to experience the sufficiency of our grace even more in the days to come. Please lead them by your Spirit along the narrow path that leads to life. May they learn to 'hang out' at our grace and mercy throne - for their sake and the sake of others needing to find the way.

Jesus

Scriptures for Grace

Hebrews 4:15-16
John 1:17
2 Corinthians 8:7-8
Ephesians 1:4-10
1 Peter 2:1-3
John 10:10-11
2 Corinthians 12:9

Grace

Dear Graced One,

Grace - unearned favor that includes kindness, comfort, benefits, pleasure, gifts and gratification. Aren't these all things that would make for happiness? While on earth, I experienced trials and temptations in the flesh (just like you) without sinning. This qualifies me to be your high priest at the throne of grace. Today, when you come boldly in faith, you obtain mercy and grace to help for any need. Our Father and I are so pleased when you choose to be the recipient and steward of this grace and mercy.

Please believe me and take advantage of this offer now. As I have told you, my grace is always sufficient and my strength is perfected in weakness. Not only are you saved by grace but true direction and deliverance are found at our grace throne. Many believe 'law abiding' to be the answer to life's problems. But it is 'Spirit confiding' that leads to the fulfilling of the law and my gift of abundance of life.

Come to our throne . We're expecting you...

Your High Priest,
Jesus

Prayer for the Happy Hearted

Awesome Father God,
Bless this happy hearted one and protect them from the arrows shot from the darkness to wound and weaken them. Reveal more and more of your hope and future for that they might set their affection on things above and what you have prepared for them because they love You.
Jesus

Happiness Scriptures

Matthew 5:14-16 & 28:20
1 Corinthians 2:9
Colossians 1:27 & 3:1-4
Philippians 4:4-7
Hebrews 12:2
2 Corinthians 4:17-18
1 Peter 1:2 & 2:19-20

Happiness

Dear Happy Heart

I love it when you choose to be happy! Like the expression 'putting the horse before the cart,' many people are happy only when their circumstances are good and they are prospering. But the happiness I offer is greater than any temporary situation - and every situation is temporary, believe it or not.

Unimaginable riches and well being - even just hearing those words of our Kingdom life hold the power to bring happiness as they quicken your spirit. And they are just two that express the reality of the Kingdom where I dwell. Peace, love, joy, purity and security - all of these are part of your inheritance as a blood bought child of the King.

'For the joy set before me, I endured the cross, despising the shame...' Being with you forever is an essential part of that joy that makes my heart happy as I hope it makes yours. The temporary, light afflictions of this life are nothing compared to the eternal abundance of glory we are to share. You glow when your thoughts dwell on this and your heart leads you to share your happiness through acts of service and words of encouragement and belief with others. Shine on!

Your happy hearted partner,

Jesus

Prayer for the Hopeful

Dear Father of Glory,
I pray that this beautiful child of yours be protected because their helmet of the hope of salvation is in place. I know they will be more than satisfied with the glory that awaits them. Their inheritance is awesome beyond their comprehension and it will last forever! I desire that they know this is what I paid for on the cross for them.
Jesus

Scriptures of Hope

Revelation 21:1-4
John 16:33
Ephesians 1:15-23 & 6:11-17
Colossians 1:27
Romans 4:12-22 & 8:17-25
Hebrews 6:10-19
1 John 3:1-3
1 Thessalonians 5:8

Hope

Dear Hopeful One,

As a boat floats, so hope keeps your life afloat. Can you hope for a life better than the one awaiting you in heaven where your tears are wiped away and there is no more death, sorrow, crying or pain? Anticipation of such a glorious life will keep you buoyant, optimistic and enthusiastic. This benefits you and those around you.

I was speaking the truth when I told you that in this world you would experience troubles and temptations. But as I endured and have overcome this world, including its pain and sorrow, so will you. In every situation, I trusted in our Father's love and power. It was exciting, rewarding and led to my resurrection into this magnificent heaven where I await your arrival.

'Christ in you, the hope of glory.' Let this hope be the anchor of your soul. You can be sure that through the storms of life, you will not only survive, but be strengthened, protected and perfected.

Glory, my glory is to be yours forever!

Truly yours,
Jesus

Prayer for the Humble

Dear Father of the Humble

Reveal to this precious child of yours how their putting on humbleness of mind gains them great honor in your Kingdom as well as winning them rest for their soul. I know it is your plan an desire to exalt them at just the right time.

Jesus

Scriptures for the Humble

Matthew 1:18-25 & 11:28-30
Luke 2:1-14
Mark 15:37-38
1 Peter 5:6
Philippians 2:8
Isaiah 57:15
Colossians 3:12-13
Matthew 18:1-6

Humble

Dear Humble Heart,

Our Father and I have noticed every time you have chosen to be humble of heart and served others, not seeking the limelight or despising others. Your ignoring the cry, 'What's in it for me?' and putting another's needs first touches our Father's heart and opens the door to His throne of grace.

Consider the humble circumstances of my birth. It was no accident. A mother rejected by law and society - impregnated with seed from God. Birth in a lowly stable - angels singing gloriously in the heavens. Death on a cross, a most humiliating form of dying - the curtain in the temple that separated the Holy of Holies from the world torn in two from the top to the bottom.

Hidden in plain and simple situations of this life is the glory of the great I AM. That glory always overshadows and overcomes the pride of life and the lusts of the eyes and the flesh.

Remember, I am humble and lowly in heart and have assured you that as you humble yourself as a little child, you become one of the greatest in the Kingdom of heaven.

Simply yours,

Jesus

Prayer for the Innocent

Dear Gracious Father,

Before the foundation of the world I saw this precious one and chose them to be with us in our Kingdom. May the truly good news of redemption and reconciliation sink into their souls and may they clearly hear and follow the leading of the Spirit in their spirit.

Jesus

Scriptures for the Innocent

Luke 23:34
Colossians 1:12-23
John 8:32-36 & 14:1-6
Romans 5:8-10
Mark 14:24
Hebrews 8:10-13, 9:14 & 12:24
2 Corinthians 5:17-18
Ephesians 1:7 & 2:13

Innocent

Dear Blameless One,

'Not guilty' is my cry before the Father of the universe on your behalf. All your mistakes - past, present and future - can be wiped off your slate if you can believe and receive it.

I was born of lowly estate, never held public office or any position of worldly fame or authority, accumulated no great possessions and was accused and sentenced to death by the religious and political leaders of my day. Nevertheless, I hold the key of welcome and acceptance for you into the Kingdom of God which holds unsurpassed beauty, riches and well being.

Receive my gift (forgiveness is its name) of freedom from the power of and the punishment for mistakes - yours and others. Take the time to allow the blood I shed on the cross to cover and cleanse you from all the things you have done to others and others have done to you that cry 'guilty' in your soul. Then partake of and enjoy reconciliation with your Father who loves you beyond your wildest dreams.

Freely and faithfully yours,

Jesus

Prayer for the Joyful

Abba Father,

Like the man who found treasure hid in a field and sold all he had to buy that field, may this beloved child of yours ever experience the joy of the kingdom of heaven in their heart until the appointed time for them to join us in our kingdom. As they abide in my love by faith, may their fruitfulness bring them fullness of joy.

Jesus

Scriptures for Joy

Hebrews 10:12-13 & 12:2
John 15:7-11 & 16:24
1 Corinthians 2:9
Luke 6:38
Matthew 13:44
Galatians 5:22
Romans 15:13
James 1:1-4
1 Peter 1:3-8 & 4:12-13

Joy

Dear Cheerful One,

Your cheerful, hopeful expectancy in any and every situation blesses our Father and me. As I am expecting until my enemies be made my footstool, so your choice to do the same makes you the light of the world.

I am ever offering my joy to you. In good times and bad, there is joy to be had. It might be the joy of forgiveness for mistakes (yours or someone else's) followed by new beginnings. It might be the joy of having your need met or having the honor of meeting another's need. It is not material substance and success that bring you lasting joy. It is all the ways love flows to and through you - caring, sharing and bearing - that make for genuine joy.

Joy lies like a treasure within the truth of the Word, sparkling like a diamond and reflecting the light of love. Bask in its beauty and rely on its strength. Ask of me according to my Word and you will experience the fullness of joy that I came to bring just for you.

Joyfully yours,

Jesus

Prayer for the Kindhearted

Dear Father of Kindness,
Bless and keep this child of yours and help them to hear your voice and follow your lead in being kind, even to those they might feel don't deserve it. Inspire and amaze them with acts of kindness to and through them that are even beyond their imagination!
Jesus

Scriptures for the Kind

Matthew 7:11-12
Luke 6:35
Romans 12:10
1 Corinthians 13:4
Ephesians 2:7 & 4:32
Colossians 3:12
2 Peter 1:5-8

Kind

Dear Kindhearted,

I love it when you are kind. Not one of your acts of kindness has gone unnoticed or unappreciated by our Father and me. Kindness is one of the attributes of love (a more excellent way) that makes for quality of love. It is also one of the ways you show yourself to be a true minister of God.

Being kind holds a blessing in it for you as well as for the one you are kind to. Forgiving, feeding a hungry crowd, healing, speaking a word of truth and encouragement - these are some of the ways the Father led me to show His kindness while I was on the earth. Gratitude and affirmation were not requirements for my kindness to be expressed. Neither do they need to be for you. But when you sow kindness, whether it be in thought, word or deed, you will reap peace of mind and health in your body. And, most important of all, your kindness demonstrates that you are a child of the Most High, who is kind to the unthankful and the evil.

What a heritage and what great rewards await you in the Kingdom of God!

Graciously yours,
Jesus

Prayer for Lovers

Dear Father of Love,

You have already shed your love abroad in this child's heart as they have endured their trials and temptations in faith. I pray they experience the joy that this love brings. May they know in their hearts the truth of my love surpassing knowledge, be filled with Your fullness and grasp just an inkling of how what You have in store for them is greater than they could even think or imagine.

Jesus

Scriptures of Love

John 3:16
Isaiah 53:4
1 Corinthians 13:1-13
John 15:10-13 & 16:24
Matthew 22:36-40
Ephesians 3:14-21
1 Peter 4:8
1 John 4:7-12

Love

Beloved,

You are loved by the Lord above all! Believe this. Receive this for it is the truth above all else.

God, your heavenly Father, loved you so much that He gave you me. I love you so much that I was willing to die once on earth rather than live without you forever. Meditate on this. Let it sink in and ask us to show you this love for we are more than willing to do so.

The giving of my life opened the door for kingdom living for you and me. For you it may start with letting me bear your pains and sorrows. Surely, I am willing to do this. Then you can partake of our riches as you accept the forgiveness I offer for your mistakes as well as others'. This will enable you to fulfill my new commandment to love one another as I have loved you.

Our Father and I love you unconditionally and without end. Even in experiences that are evil, our love is present to rescue and redeem, to bear with and bless you. Let it!

All my love forever and ever,

Jesus

Prayer for the Meek

Abba Father,

I know you are looking forward to this child of yours receiving their inheritance. Truly, 'the meek shall inherit the earth' and I so look forward to your exalting this meek one at just the perfect time!

Jesus

Scriptures for the Meek

Matthew 5:5 & 11:28-30
Galatians 5:22-23
Ephesians 4:1-3
Colossians 3:12
James 1:21 & 3:13
1 Peter 3:4
Psalms 149:4
Proverbs 15:1

Meekness

Beloved,

Your gentle, quiet countenance is a beautiful thing. Though, in the world, meekness might be equated with weakness, it is an attitude and attribute that is of great value in God's sight. It is not the contentious and controlling that shall ultimately 'inherit the earth,' but the gentle and humble who follow me and honor God's will and ways.

So many expected me to be a conqueror with armies marching to victory over the evils of the day. It was success, not sacrifice that they thought would make for freedom. But it was and still is in learning of my meek and quiet heart that you will find rest for your own soul and true victory with its everlasting rewards that your heavenly Father has in store for you.

As a soft answer turns away wrath, so your meekness will be peace and power producing, inside and out, in this world and the one to come (which lasts forever).

Your Peace Provider,
Jesus

Prayer for the Merciful

Dear Lord Above All,
Please let this precious child of yours know they are welcome at your throne of grace and may the Holy Spirit encourage them to come often for we are waiting for them. You truly crown their life with loving kindness and tender mercies as they choose not to forget your most awesome benefit package.
Let them know that I have paid their premium.
Jesus

Scriptures for the Merciful

Matthew 5:7 & 12:7
Mark 11:25
James 2:13
Hebrews 4:16
Matthew 9:27-29
Luke 6:35-37
Psalm 103:1-4

Mercy

Dear Merciful One,

Thank you for choosing to be merciful. Your acts of mercy have never gone unnoticed by our Father or me. Even when others and your own heart have condemned your act of mercy, there is cheering in heaven from the cloud of witnesses and a beaming of the ever present light in the heart of God.

Blessed, not cursed, are those who show mercy to those who need it. And that mercy not only holds the thanks of the recipient but the promise of blessing from the God above all gods. He made it clear in the Word that no mercy will be shown to those who show no mercy and that, ultimately, mercy will triumph over judgment.

Mercy magnified - judgment satisfied. That is what my life and death on earth was and still is all about. Now I am available as your high priest at the throne of grace where you can come boldly and you WILL obtain mercy and find grace in your time of need. You can also come when you are interceding for someone else's need. You have our word on it.

Your Advocate at the Mercy Seat,

Jesus

Prayer for the Noble

Dear Father of Nobility,
I know you are aware of every time this child of yours offered themselves as a living sacrifice. Though the world has ignored or even belittled these acts at times, I stand with them expecting their awesome reward in heaven.
Jesus

Scriptures for the Noble

1 John 3:16
Luke 14:11 & 18:9-14
John 15:13
Luke 21:1-4
Romans 2:21-29
1 Peter 5:5-7
Hebrews 12:2

Noble

Dear Excellent One,

You are noble in my sight. I have noticed every time you have sacrificed your own desires for obedience to mine or the benefit of another. I was pleased when you gave up personal gratification and chose to do what you knew in your heart was right.

In the long run (and eternity is longer than you can imagine), it doesn't really matter what people think. Their praise or criticism isn't the bottom line. I continually had to pay attention and follow the leading of our Father rather than what my friends and enemies were saying or doing. Nobility of character disregards the opinions of people and personal advantage. It is faithful to the higher law of love and truth within.

When you do your best and give your all, you are a hero to the cloud of witnesses watching from heaven. Remember, what the world might despise often is what is highly prized by your heavenly Father and me. Count on it.

Respectfully yours,
Jesus

Prayer for the Overcomer

Dear Rewarder of the Overcomer,
Thank you for sending your Holy Spirit to help this precious child of yours to be victorious in their times of trial and temptation. May my words and works, which are spirit and life, serve them well in becoming overcomers in this life and citizens of the Kingdom of heaven forever.
Jesus

Scriptures for the Overcomer

Matthew 4:1-11
Mark 8:34-38
Luke 6:38 & 22:39-46
John 6:63 & 14:6
1 Corinthians 2:9 & 10:1-6
Hebrews 11:6
Revelations 3:20-21

Overcomer

Dear Overcoming One,

I am honored and blessed when you overcome the temptation to give up or give in. Your love for, joy in and obedience to me is priceless. While your own good deeds and great words may bring temporary recognition and reward at best, your belief in me as your way, your truth and your life produces everlasting approval and and rewards.

The opportunity and challenge to overcome was ever present for me while lived on the earth. It was my love for the Father and my faith in His plan, including its beginning, middle and end, that kept me useful to Him and free from the rebellion and wrath of my enemy. I have no regrets.

Now you have no idea how great the reward is for enduring to the end. Give, not up or in, but all you have in my name. Believe me when I tell you there is no greater, more lasting or desirable reward than the one I am preparing for you.

Blessings Above Measure to You,

Jesus

Prayer for the Patient

Dear Father of Patience,
Thank you for giving this precious child to me to keep and endue with my faith and patience. May the Holy Spirit, the spirit of truth, continue to strengthen and help them to patiently endure and experience the love of God shed abroad in their heart.
Jesus

Scriptures for the Patient

Matthew 24:13
Luke 21:19
John 16:33
Romans 2:6-7 & 5:1-5
1 Corinthians 13:4-13
Hebrews 6:12
James 1:1-4

Patience

Dear Patient One,

Your cheerful, hopeful enduring in the trials of your life is worth more than silver and gold in the Kingdom of God. In God's eyes, you are well on the way to perfection as you choose faith, hope and love over the world's darkness, despair and doubt.

You may have heard it said, 'Don't ask for patience!' supposing that you will be bound for trouble. But I told you, when I lived on earth, that 'in your patience (not works, wisdom or wealth) you possess your soul.'

Even in the doubts, denial and eventual desertion of my disciples, I chose to be patient and believe. I believed in our Father's plan, power and forgiveness more than what I saw or experienced. I encourage and cheer you on as you do the same in your life.

Endure to the end that you may be whole and healthy, safe and sound. Soon we will be forever together with no stormy weather - I can't wait!

Expectantly yours,

Jesus

Prayer for Peace

Dear Peace Producing Papa,
As you dwell in your rest, having ceased from your works, may this peaceful one partake of our promise and enter into the sabbath rest you have prepared for them. May they know the reality of our peace which surpasses understanding that we offer to guard their hearts when they choose not to worry but pray and trust us instead.
Jesus

Scriptures for Peace

Matthew 5:8 & 44-48
Matthew 18:3-4
Luke 23:46
John 14:27
Philippians 4:6-7
Hebrews 4:9-12
1 John 4:7-8
Psalm 91:1-2

Peace

Dear Peaceful One,

I have peace for you. The peace that is the result of praying and trusting absolutely your heavenly Father whose love for you is unconditional and unending. It is His greatest desire to spend eternity with you. His heart is pure and His ways are honest and good (though not always logical or in agreement with the reasoning of your natural mind).

I trusted Him with my very life and those He gave to me to disciple. I died on a cross and my disciples scattered temporarily but that was NOT the end for them or me. And you can be sure that whatever trial you go through, no matter what it looks like in the middle, your faith in your Father and His plan and His saving power (through me) will bring you to peace and abundant, eternal life.

Choose to dwell in the place of childlikeness where you completely trust your heavenly Father. Be one with me. Love all, including the unlovely, and do what is good in His sight no matter what others may say or do. It is in this place that the power to calm the tempest within and without is always found. Remember, 'Blessed are the peacemakers, for they shall be called the sons (and daughters) of God.

Be Still and Believe,

Jesus

Prayer for the Qualified

Dear Creator of Heaven and Earth,
It was our idea to make this beautiful child and I know how much you love our 'idea.' There is no one exactly like them who can do what we've ordained for them to do. I want them to know that we are more than willing and able to see them through to the victory and abundant life we've prepared for them.
Jesus

Scriptures for the Qualified

Genesis 1:26
Matthew 5:3-16
John 15:5-8 & 16
Ephesians 2:10
Romans 8:1-2 & 28-29
1 Corinthians 13:13
Ephesians 3:17-21
1 John 4:7-8

Qualified

Dear Competent One,

You were created with a purpose by the Father of all creation. He is love and He qualifies you as the focal point and instrument of that love. You have experienced many successes and failures in your life. Yet the unique thing is that each one of them - the good, the bad and the ugly - has provided you with the opportunity to receive your Father's love and grow in it. He's not in the condemning business. His goal has always been to make you in our image and to enjoy your company forever.

You are His chosen one and are qualified as a citizen of the Kingdom of heaven to love and be loved in this world and the next. In that one quality is the essence of His purpose and the fulfillment of your joy. Though you may not have qualified for some of the honors and prizes awarded on earth by people, as you obey that command of ours to love as we have and still love you, honor and glory beyond your imagination will be yours. Come to me to know the surpassing greatness of that love.

You qualify!

Jesus

Prayer for the Rewarded One

Dear Father of Bounty,

Bless this faithful child of yours with the assurance that I have overcome the world and will provide them with the strength to resist temptation so they don't have to choose pleasure for a moment over the life, light and love of your eternal Kingdom that is in their heart now and will soon be their place of residence forever with us.

Jesus

Rewarding Scriptures

Matthew 5:10-11 & 39, 6:1-6 & 19-21
John 14:6
Romans 5:1-5
Hebrews 11:6
1 Peter 1:3-4
Psalm 16:11
Psalm 103:1-6

Rewarding

Dear Rewarded One,

Thank you for seeking and finding the love of our Father. The author of Hebrews wrote, 'Without faith it is impossible to please God; for he that comes to God must believe that He is and that He is a rewarder of them that diligently seek Him.' He spoke of a faithful relationship here, not just fulfilling principles gained from the knowledge of good and evil.

It is the God centered, not the self centered life that wins. Turning the other cheek, suffering reproach for my sake, fasting and giving in secret are real winners from our perspective as is your obedience to all of my commands in the Gospels. You can be sure that we have noticed and are pleased every single time you have chosen me as your way, your truth and your life. This choosing gains you the benefit package of Psalm 103 which includes forgiveness, healing, redemption from destruction, loving kindness and tender mercy, rejuvenating and vindication.

The pleasure of worldly fame and fortune is only temporary at best while the rewards promised by our Father are incorruptible, undefiled and will never fade away but last forever. I meant it when I told you to store up treasure in heaven rather than on earth, for you will surely find that our rewards bring you fullness of joy and pleasures evermore.

Faithfully and Joyfully Yours,

Jesus

Prayer for Security

Dear Father of Safe Keeping,
I know that you are able to keep this child you love so dearly through the storms they experience in this life. May they continue to grow bolder and stronger as they put their trust in me and the leading of the Spirit of truth rather than the deceiver and tempter of man.
Jesus

Scriptures for Security

Matthew 28:20
John 15:4-7 & 16:33
Acts 10:38
1 Corinthians 13:1-13
Colossians 2:18-19
Philippians 4:6-8
Hebrews 4:9-12, 8:10-12 & 13:5-6
Revelation 1:8

Security

Beloved,

I am with you always - bearing, believing, hoping and enduring with you, in you and for you. I can rescue you from whatever destructive pit you have been or are in. Our benefit plan that is presented to you in Psalm 103 has better benefits than any insurance policy you can find and the price couldn't be better - faith in me that I have paid it in full for you.

Believe me when I tell you that I have overcome the world. The past, present and future are surely in my hands. Take possession of this truth for it will provide security like nothing else. I can see the beginning and the end, but, truly, I am with you on the journey from one to the other.

This is not only true for you but also for those you love and pray for. I can reveal myself to them as uniquely as I have revealed myself to you. As you continue to pray for them as I lead you and trust them to me for safe keeping, both of you can partake of the peace I offer that surpasses understanding. Believe and enter into the sabbath rest I have for you.

Faithfully yours,

Jesus

Prayer for the Tender Hearted

Dear Loving Father,
The tender heart of this one so dear to you is beautiful. May they ever remain sensitive to and a vessel of your love and leading until I come for them and we dwell in your house together forever.
Jesus

Scriptures for the Tender Hearted

Matthew 26:69-75
Mark 1:40-42
Luke 21:19 & 10:30-37
John 8:3-11
1 Corinthians 13:4
2 Corinthians 4:17-18
Galatians 6:2
1 Peter 3:8

Tender Hearted

Dear Caring One,

I appreciate your tender heart that is willing to be touched by the needs and pains of others. Your choice to be patient and kind in trying circumstances makes you a delight to the heart of God while it offers those on earth an opportunity to sample my goodness.

When I walked on the earth, you could witness my heart condition. I fed the hungry, forgave the woman caught in sin and looked into Peter's eyes without condemnation as he denied me in front of my enemies.

Perhaps you have been advised to use 'tough love' in order to right a wrong or just stand for what you know is right. Surely, your 'yes' should be 'yes' and your 'no' a real 'no.' However, your willingness to offer your life as a vessel of my love and forgiveness will produce unsurpassed fulfillment for you and as well as me. Beyond the temporary pain of rejection or apparent failure lies the Father's praise and prize. Both of these are permanent and they are waiting for you, dear tender hearted one.

Look up!

Compassionately and Courageously yours,

Jesus

Prayer for the Thankful

Abba Father,
I know what joy it brings You when this precious one gives you thanks in difficult as well as pleasant situations. I so want them to experience Your presence and power at all times , just the way Paul and Silas did when they were thrown into prison.
May it be so!
Jesus

Scriptures for the Thankful

Matthew 8:2-3 & 9:20-22
Luke 23:46
John 11:41-44
Acts 16:14-34
Ephesians 5:19-21
Hebrews 12:1-2
Psalm 100:1-5

Thankful

Dear Grateful One,

Thank you for being thankful. Being a vessel of thanksgiving is beautiful beyond description in the Kingdom of God. It is an expression of your love that touches your Father's heart in a very special way. Your trust brings His power on the scene to deliver you from evil, whatever it may be. How many times while I was on earth did I demonstrate that a needy one's faith in me had made them whole?

I thanked the Father for hearing me as I stood before Lazarus' grave, believing resurrection was His plan. But I also lifted my eyes to heaven when the hour had come to glorify our Father by my going to the cross. Now I sit at our Father's right hand where I am interceding and expecting.

Paul was speaking on our behalf when he told believers to give thanks **for all things** always to the Father in my name. Truly, as you enter His gates with thanksgiving in your heart and His courts with praise, we are one and you are the fulfillment of the joy set before me that led me to endure the cross. And it will be confirmed to you that He is good and His mercy is everlasting.

Thanks for being thankful,

Jesus

Prayer for the Understanding

Dear Understanding Father,
Your Kingdom is already within this precious one's heart. May they find joy and contentment in the understanding this provides their heart as long as they are in this world. And may they grow daily in their expectancy of my return for them. I so look forward to being with them forever and seeing them receive Your rewards for their understanding Your will and acting upon it.
Jesus

Scriptures for Understanding

Matthew 11:15-19 & 13:13-17
Mark 11:24-26
Luke 8:4-15
John 13:34-35 & 14:1-14
Romans 8:15-18
Ephesians 1:16-23

Understanding

Beloved,

Understand: to comprehend the meaning of, to accept as established. Many times I spoke of people hearing but not understanding. Many just did not grasp the truth of my words or believe that I meant what I said. Others let the troubles of this world or its pleasures be their focus. You are so wise when you accept as truth my words and direction and live your life based on them.

My goal is not to stump you so that you give up or in but rather to help you find the path that leads to life everlasting and the place I prepared just for you. Forget what others are doing and look to me and be led exclusively by the Spirit of God, not the wisdom of men. My words like, 'don't judge, forgive and love as I have loved you,' are words worth apprehending and acting on every day.

The sufferings of this world pale in comparison to the glory of His Kingdom. It is our Father's desire and purpose to open the eyes of your understanding more and more to his glory, riches and power which are always full of His love and never fade away.

Ask Him to!

Jesus

Prayer for the Victor

Dear Creator-Sustainer,
We knew this child before the foundation of the world and all their days have been written in your book and the hairs on their head are numbered. I am praying that their faith fail not and that they will strengthen their brothers and sisters on the earth.
Jesus

Scriptures for Victory

Matthew 6:25-30, 10:28-31 & 25:34
Luke 18:9-14 & 22;32
John 10:27-30 & 15:16
Romans 8:1-4 & 28-30
2 Corinthians 12:9-10
Psalm 139:13-18
John 17:20-26

Victory

Dear Victorious One,

You are so precious in my sight. You are my beloved and that is above and beyond all that real and all circumstances here on earth. From my perspective worldly successes and failures are irrelevant. There is life offered at all times. What are failures in the world's eyes are opportunities in mine. I only refine and prune. I never have destruction or condemnation in mind.

You belong to me and the path I have for you to walk is forward and upward. My grace and provision are **always** sufficient. I long to take care of you as our Father and I have promised; just the way we take care of the birds of the air and the lilies of the field.

Through the Spirit, I will show you things to come , things that even the prophets and angels have not seen. I also desire to use you in ways you cannot imagine (so don't even try to). I have overcome the world. All you need to do is trust me and be brave. The best is definitely yet to come! You might sing a chorus of 'Victory in Jesus' for I am your Savior forever.

And I'll love you just as long!
Jesus

Prayer for My Winner

Dear Rewarder in Heaven,
May this winner in your book continue to watch for my return and anticipate the rewards you have for them for diligently seeking You. As they set their affection on the place I've prepared for them and their being with us forever, I will keep them in our special peace and love that surpass anything the god of this world has to offer.
Jesus

Scriptures for My Winner

John 10:27-30
John 14:1-6
John 15:16 & 16:33
Romans 8:28-30
1 Corinthians 15:55-58
Ephesians 2:10
Colossians 3:1-4
Hebrews 11:6

Winner

Dear Chosen One,

You are a born winner - chosen by me to bring forth fruit that will last forever. I know there have been blights and pests in your life that would damage or destroy your fruit if that were possible, but it is not! There is no dis-appointment that can prevail over my 'appointment' of you for there is no power greater than that of our Father and He and I are one.

You are unique and precious to us beyond your wildest imagination. Your trials and tribulations (which I said you would experience) can only refine, not ruin you. Think of the baker who grinds the flour, beats the eggs, adds the yeast, mixes them all together and then waits for the rising power to be complete. Then he puts his creation in a hot oven for just the right amount of time, his eye on the product rather than the process.

Now think of me, the true bread of life, and rejoice! Our vision for you is divine and your victory secure.

You are the joy of my life,

Jesus

Prayer for the Expectant One

Dear Father,
I pray for this child-in-waiting. Though they can't see in the natural how awesome your Kingdom really is and what riches and well being await them, may their faith flourish as they focus on all your promises. And may they join me as I continue to expect until all my enemies are under my feet.
Jesus

Scriptures for Expecting

Mark 1:14-15
John 14:1-3
1 Corinthians 2:9
Hebrews 9:28 & 10:12-14
James 1:12
Revelations 21:1-27
Isaiah 40:31

eXpecting

Dear Promised One,

I am coming again, just as I have promised you. As surely as a mother enters her 'expecting' mode when she is told she is 'with child,' I declare that you can expect a life with me, above and beyond your greatest imagination in our Father's Kingdom. May you look forward to my arrival today and every day, for I am coming a second time for those who are looking for me.

Just now, I am waiting. My sacrifice has been made and I am seated at the right hand of our Father expecting until my enemies be made my footstool. I know that you are waiting too. But, remember that the Lord renews the strength of those who wait upon Him and He has a crown of life as your reward for your enduring love of Him. Continue to be of good cheer at the thought of our being together forever. As a mother-to-be takes special care of herself for the benefit of her unborn child, you, as a new creation in me, can prepare yourself for this new life. Pay attention to my words and life on earth and walk in the spirit as the Holy Spirit leads you.

Don't give up! Let my love of you and in you overcome any present darkness. Anticipate living in our Kingdom where there is no night but awesome, never ending light!

In joyful anticipation,

Jesus

Prayer for the Young at Heart

Dear Father of the Fountain of Youth,
Here is a true child of yours whose faith has failed not. Instead, their heart is full of the faith that You are looking for and pleases You. May they experience fullness of joy as they taste of your rewards here on earth and anticipate the everlasting ones awaiting them in heaven.
Jesus

Scriptures for the Young at Heart

Matthew 7:24-25
Matthew 8:5-10 & 18:3-4
1 Corinthians 2:9
Luke 9:46-48
Luke 18:1-8 & 15-17
Hebrews 11:6
1 Peter 5:6-7
Isaiah 40:31

Young at Heart

Dear Child of the King,

I am so blessed when you listen to me and follow in my footsteps of unwavering love and trust in our awesome Father. Your willingness to be childlike in obedience to what we have told you to do, trusting the outcome to Him, is the true fountain of youth. He wants you to be care free. And you can be as you live as His child and dwell in His love.

The simple trust of a child playing happily in the presence of their watchful and wise parent brings joy and delight to the parent as well as the observer. How impressed and pleased I was by the faith and trust of the centurion who knew not only authority's power but the heart of a good authority for the well being of those under him. It was a pleasure to have my healing virtue flow to his servant.

As you choose to stay hopeful and alive to new possibilities and adventures, regardless of your age or circumstances, you bring pleasure to all in the Kingdom of Heaven.

'Perfect!' is the response of our Father when you give your all to do what He has written in your heart and His word. Rejoice in His praise and protection, dear youthful one.

Jesus

Prayer for Those with Zest

Dear Father of Abundant Life,
This precious one of yours has benefited rather than being beaten down or taken captive by the trials of their life. Now our love has been poured out and is abiding in their heart and they share it with others. Guide and sustain them as they continue lighting up the world and setting people free.
Jesus

Scriptures for Zest

Matthew 8:8-13 & 15:22-28
Luke 18:1-8
John 1:12-13 & 10:10 & 27-30
John 16:33
Romans 8:28-30 & 9:22-23
1 Corinthians 2:9
Ephesians 1:3-14
Psalm 16:11

Zest

Dear Lively One,

Your zest for life can never be defeated or destroyed. That is because you are a child of the King whose Kingdom is full of gusto with a capital G! Just as a cork always pops back up to the top of the water after it has been held down by force, so shall you survive and thrive, very much alive, from the trials and tribulations of this life. My overcoming of the world has gained that for you.

Our Father and I love when you stay faith-filled and thankful - knowing all things work for good in making you more like me. Like the centurion who sought me for his servant's healing and the woman from Canaan who knew I could help her daughter who was oppressed by a devil, your 'only believing' will reap awesome results not only here on earth but in heaven where results last forever.

Nothing is stronger than the Father's love for you that dwells in me. His love and power raised me from the grave. That's zest at its best! Seek and enjoy our presence and wisdom. Be exhilarated by thoughts of the riches of the glory and mansion I've prepared just for you.

Truly, the best is yet to come!

The Beginning and The End,

Jesus

Love Letters from Jesus

The love of Jesus truly surpasses knowledge. As He is the source of life for every believing person, so the countless expressions of that love can lift and feed our spirits like nothing else. Hopefully, these letters have blessed and encouraged you in experiencing His love a little more at just the right time.

The letters are available as a pad, cards or individual inserts as well as in this book form. If you would like to know how to obtain them so you can pass on His love this way-

Please contact me at:

spiritandlifelighters@gmail.com

Sally F. Boenau